Grand Book of Trivia

Peter Joseph

DEDICATION

This book is dedicated to my family, first to my wife Andrea,who has been so tolerant with me over the years. My children: Orion and his wife Alicia, Adrian, Damien and his wife Anna, Lauren and her husband Josiah. My Grandchildren: Alex, Maiya,Airi, Anya,Trysten and Elena. All of them are my inspiration and my heroes. Through them, I find, living in this very complicated world less stressful.

LEVELS OF DIFFICULTY

1 EASIEST

1. Who is NOT one of Tom Hank's children?
1. Elizabeth
2. Truman
3. Edward
4. Colin

2. What is the brightest star in the Orion Constellation?
1. Antares
2. Spica
3. Rigel
4. Capella

3. Lori "Lolo" Jones is a track and field athlete who also competes in what other Olympic sport?
1. Archery
2. Skiing
3. Bobsledding
4. Gymnastics

DID YOU KNOW: The city of Murfreesboro, Tennessee lies in the exact geographical center of the state

4. Journalist Geraldo Rivera hosted a documentary which fleedopped in 1986. What was the name of the documentary?

    1. Versailles Opening,

    2. Al capone's Vault,

    3. Venice Findings,

    4. King Tuts Tomb

5. On the show Friends, which guest star left Chandler stranded in a restaurant restroom wearing only pink underwear?

    1.Meg Ryan

    2. Angelina Jolie

    3. Julia Roberts,

    4. Christina Applegate

6.Which country has the longest coastline in the world?

    1.Canada

    2. Japan

    3. Indonesia

    4. China

7.What would be found in an impluvium in ancient Roman home?

    1. Water

    2. Perfume

    3. Oil

    4. Wine

DID YOU KNOW: Iceland boasts the world's oldest functioning legislative assembly, the Althing, established in 930.

8.King Henry the Eighth had how many wives?
  1. Six
  2. Eight
  3. Four
  4. Two

9.Which artist had a hit with "Call me Maybe"?
  1. Adele
  2. Katy Perry
  3. Carly Rae Jepsen
  4. Lady Gaga

10.What year was the Etch A Sketch introduced to the public?
  1. 1950
  2. 1980
  3. 1960
  4. 1940

11.Where is the famous Piazza San Marco?
  1. Rome
  2. Venice
  3. Madrid
  4. Barcelona

12. How old did Rolling Stones singer Mick Jagger turn in July 2013?
  1. 80
  2. 70
  3. 60
  4. 65

13. What was jazz musician Miles Davis' middle name?

    1. Hewey   3. Stewey

    2. Louie   4. Dewey

14. In Disney's 'Alice in Wonderland', what numbers are on the Mad Hatter's hat?

    1. 20 and

    2. 15 and 3

    3. 10 and 6

    4. 14 and 4

15. What is a baby porcupine called?

    1. Porcupette

    2. Porcupie

    3. Porcuphilly

    4. Porcupup

16. In the hit show Breaking Bad, Walter Jr. only eats which types of foods?

    1. Vegetables

    2. Lunch

    3. Breakfast

    4. Dinner

DID YOU KNOW: The average snowfall in the mountains near Salt Lake City, Utah is 500 inches

17. In 2005, who did Forbes magazine list as America's richest fictional character, with an infinite estimated net worth?
  1. Santa Claus
  2. Scrooge McDuck
  3. Richie Rich
  4. Lex Luthor

18. In billiards, what's the term for accidental contact between balls that causes a shot to fail?
  1. Kiss-Out
  2. Boomer
  3. Loop Hit
  4. Sinker

19. What kind of degree does someone with LL.B. after their name hold?
  1. Law
  2. Arts
  3. Engineering
  4. Medicine

20. Where are the cricket's eardrums located?
  1. Wings
  2. Knees
  3. Forehead
  4. Antennae

DID YOU KNOW: Sweden has not participated in any war in almost two centuries

21. Where does a stevedore work?
1. Courtroom
2. Dock
3. Hospital
4. School

22. Gala, Jonagold and Pink Lady are varieties of which fruit?
1. Apple
2. Cherry
3. Banana
4. Pear

23. Who wrote the poem 'The Owl and the Pussycat'?
1. Stephen King
2. Edward Lear
3. David Myers
4. Agatha Christie

24. Which organ of the body is affected by Bright's Disease?
1. Skin
2. Kidney
3. Heart
4. Lungs

DID YOU KNOW: Elk Horn in the state of Iowa is the largest Danish settlement in the United States.

25. What color is the bulls eye on a standard dartboard?
1. Red
2. Black
3. Green
4. Orange

DID YOU KNOW: Pitch Lake, on Trinidad and Tobago southwestern coast, is the world's largest natural reservoir of asphalt

2. EASY

26. What was the 1st human invention that broke the sound barrier?
      1. The airplane
      2. The Rocket
      3. The Train
      4. The Whip

27. How many rounds are there in an Olympic boxing match?
      1. 2-Two
      2. 4-Four
      3. 6-Six
      4. 8-Eight

28. What is the largest fresh water lake in North America?
      1. Lake Michigan
      2. Lake Ontario
      3. Lake Superior
      4. Lake Huron

DID YOU KNOW: The town of Fort Atkinson ,Iowa was the site of the only fort ever built by the U.S. government to protect one Indian tribe from another.

29. Which South American country was named after the Italian city of Venice?

    1. Columbia

    2. Venezuela

    3. Trinidad

    4. Brazil

30. What is the boiling point of water using the scientific kelvin scale of temperature measurement?

    1. 212k

    2. 312k

    3. 373k

    4. 462k

31.The round table was given to King Arthur after his marriage to who?

    1. Isolde

    2. Elaine the fair

    3. Guinevere

    4. Morgana Le Fay

32. What was the name of Taco Bell's Chihuahua mascot?

    1. Mia   3. Foxy

    2. Lola   4. Gidget

DID YOU KNOW: The first professional baseball game was played in Fort Wayne, Indiana on May 4, 1871.

33. The first long-distance auto race in the U. S. was held May 30 , in what year?
>   1. 1911
>   2. 1920
>   3. 1926
>   4. 1932

34. Marcella Gruelle of Indianapolis created the Raggedy Ann doll in what year?
>   1. 1918
>   2. 1914
>   3. 1935
>   4. 1950

35. In what city in United States was actor James Dean born?
>   1. Chicago, Illinois
>   2. Brooklyn, New York
>   3. Marion, Indiana
>   4. Omaha, Nebraska

36. Which of these birds most commonly provided the quills for quill pens?
>   1. Pigeons
>   2. Chicken
>   3. Peacocks
>   4. Geese

DID YOU KNOW: Iowa is the only US state name that starts with two vowels

37. In an average day, a person's heart beats approx. how many times

    1. 50,000   3. 75,000

    2. 100,000   4. 150,000

38. How long does it take food to travel from the mouth to the stomach via the esophagus?

    1. 5 seconds

    2. 6 seconds

    3. 7 seconds

    4. 10 seconds

39. Which constellation is known as The Hunter?

    1. Orion

    2. Sagittarius

    3. Taurus

    4. Pisces

40. What does a butterfly use to taste with?

    1. Antennae

    2. Feet

    3. Mouth

    4. Wings

41. A dog has 4 toes on their hind feet, how many toes are on their front feet?

    1. 3-Three

    2. 4-Four

    3. 5-Five

    4. 6-Six

DID YOU KNOW: The US state Indiana means, "Land of the Indians"

42. What is pregnant goldfish called?

1. Mamafish　　　　　　3. Twit
2. Preggy　　　　　　　4. Ladygue

43. What is the official nickname of the state of California?

1. Sunshine
2. Orange
3. Golden
4. Garden

44. How many dots are there on a typical pair of 6-sided dice?

1. 22
2. 42
3. 26
4. .44

45. The world's first skyscraper was built in what USA city?

1. New York
2. Chicago
3. Los Angeles
4. Detroit

46. Where on the body would a ruff be worn?

1. Wrist
2. Ankle
3. Neck
4. Waist

DID YOU KNOW: The first Aquarium opened in Chicago,Illinois in 1893

47. Who was the first man in space?
1. Neil Armstrong
2. Buzz Aldrin
3. Yuri Gagarin
4. Scott Altman

48. Which of these beans is usually used to make canned baked beans?
1. Butter
2. Haricot
3. Soy
4. Garbanzo

49. What nationality was Marco Polo?
1. Spanish
2. Italian
3. Mexican
4. Russian

50. What does Crayola mean
1. Oily Chalk,
2. Pretty Chalk,
3. Different Colors
4. Writing Colors

DID YOU KNOW: There are only 12 letters in the Hawaiian alphabet. Vowels: A, E, I, O, U ,Consonants: H, K, L, M, N, P, W

3 MEDIUM

51. The food chain Taco Bell was named after which bell?
　　1. Juan Bell
　　2. Glen Bell
　　3. Jose Bell
　　4. George Bell

52. Who's picture is on the USA $500 bill?
　　1. William McKinley,
　　2. James Madison,
　　3. Thomas Jefferson,
　　4. Grover Cleveland

53. Who's picture is on the USA $1,000 bill
　　1. Thomas Jefferson,
　　2. Grover Cleveland,
　　3. James Madison,
　　4. Thomas Jefferson

54. Who's picture is on the USA $5,000 bill?
　　1. Abraham Lincoln,
　　2. Thomas Jefferson,
　　3. James Madison,
　　4. William McKinley

DID YOU KNOW: In 1888, "Honest Dick" Tate the Kentucky state treasurer embezzled $247,000 and fled the state.

55. Who is the month of July named after?
1. Julia Riva
2. Julius Ceasar
3. Julio Escava
4. Judy Garter

56. What was the favorite song of Ross Geller's pet Capuchin monkey, Marcel, on the TV sitcom Friends?
1. The lion sleeps tonight,
2. Monkeyman,
3. Brass Monkey,
4. Kakuta Matata

57. According to Ripley's Believe It or Not, Burlington's Snake Alley in the state of Iowa has the title of
1. The shortest road in the world
2. The longest alley in the world
3. The most crooked street in the world
4. The street with the most lights

58. Who created the charactefather?
1. Zeus   3. Hades
2. Apollo   4. Eros

62. In Greek mythology, who kidnapped Persephone?
1. Zeus
2. Apollo
3. Hades
4. Artemis

63. In the movie twilight, what is Bella's full name?

    1. Isabella Katherine Swan

    2. Isabella Naomi Swan

    3. Isabella Marie Swan

    4. Isabella Adele Swan

64. Which is not a traditional ingredient in the Scottish dish Rumbledethumps?

    1. Rice

    2. Potato

    3. Cabbage

    4. Onions

65. When it comes to two-letter Internet country codes, .us stands for the United States. What country is represented by .es?

    1. Equador

    2. Estonia

    3. Spain

    4. Europa Island

66. What was the first Space Shuttle called? Hint - it was not built for space missions.

    1. Endeavor   3. Challanger

    2. Enterprise   4. Apollo

67. One of these things is not like the others. Which is it?

    1. Rambutan

    2. Sweetsop

    3. Cherimoya

    4. Kokopu

68. In what state is the oldest European settlement in North America?

    1. New York

    2. Maryland

    3. Florida

    4. Pennsylvania

69. Which is the southernmost state in the United States ?

    1. Florida

    2. Texas

    3. Mexico

    4. Hawaii

70. What festival is celebrated in Niceville, Florida every year on the third weekend in October?

    1. King Mango Strut

    2. Boggy Bayou Mullet

    3. Avon heritage Duct Tape

    4. Half Moon Bay Art and Pumpkin

71. Gatorade is named after which USA University?

    1. University of Louisiana

    2. University of Iowa

    3. University of Illinois

    4. University of Florida

DID YOU KNOW: Middlesboro ,Kentucky is the only city in the United States built within a meteor crater

72. Plant City, the Winter Strawberry Capital of the World, holds the Guinness record for the world's largest strawberry shortcake. The 827 square-foot, 6,000-pound cake was made in what year at McCall Park?

1. 2001
2. 1999
3. 2004
4. 2005

73. The Morikami Museum and Japanese Gardens are the only museum in the United States dedicated exclusively to the living culture of Japan. What city are they located in?

1. Delray Beach
2. New York City
3. Los Angeles
4. Detroit

74. How many miles of local waterway does Fort Lauderdale, which is known as the Venice of America, have?

1. 200
2. 100
3. 150
4. 185

75. What city has the title of being billed as the Sports fishing Capital of the World?

1. Baton Rouge
2. Key West
3. Islamorada
4. Daytona Beach

4 PRETTY HARD

76. What city is known as the Dive capital of the world?
1. Bahamas
2. Key West
3. Key Largo
4. San Francisco Bay

77. In the United States, which state has two rivers with the same name- "Withlacoochee?"
1. Mississippi
2. Illinois
3. Michigan
4. Florida

78. In what state was Sam Houston, arguably the most famous Texan, actually born?
1. Texas
2. Virginia
3. Tennessee
4. Florida

79. Which state is home to Dell and Compaq computers?
1. California
2. Texas
3. Maryland
4. Delaware

DID YOU KNOW: Mutual of Omaha Corporate headquarters in Nebraska is a public building built with 7 floors underground

80. The drink Dr Pepper was invented in Waco, Texas in what year?
1. 1876
2. 1885
3. 1905
4. 1925

81. In Scrabble, the letters X and J are both worth how many points?
1. Eight
2. Four
3. Six
4. Ten

81-a. In the 1994 Hollywood thriller Speed, what speed must a Los Angeles bus maintain to avoid detonating a bomb?
1. 85mph
2. 70mph
3. 50mph
4. 30mph

82. The world's smallest church measuring 3.5' x 6'can be found in what state?
1. Florida
2. Michigan
3. Wyoming
4. New York

DID YOU KNOW: The first woman mayor in the United States was Susan Madora Salter. She was elected to office in Argonia, Kansas in 1887

83. The first presentation of 3D films before a paying audience took place at Manhattan's Astor Theater in what year?

      1. 1965   3. 1945

      2. 1915   4. 1996

84. The first Boy's Club was established in New York City in what year?

      1. 1899

      2. 1910

      3. 1925

      4. 1876

85. The term "the big apple" is a phrase originally coined by what group?

      1. Musicians

      2. Bank Owners

      3. Politicians

      4. Actors

86. Where is the U.S. Astronaut Hall of Fame located?

      1. Houston, TX

      2. Huntsville, AL

      3. Titusville, FL

      4. Washington, DC

DID YOU KNOW: Gold is the official state mineral of Alaska

87. Which of these words cannot be rhymed with any other English word?

    1. Rule

    2. Arm

    3. Olive

    4. Moth

88. Which state has the notorious title of the car theft capital of the world?

    1. New Jersey

    2. New York

    3. Los Angeles

    4. Michigan

89. Where is the largest seaport in the United States?

    1. Norfolk, VA

    2. Savannah, GA

    3. Elizabeth, NJ

    4. Long Beach, CA

90. Fort Dix is named for Major General John Adams Dix, a veteran of the War of?

    1. 1865

    2. 1812

    3. 1835

    4. 1896

91. The first Indian Reservation was set up in what state?

    1. Florida

    2. Tennessee

    3. New Jersey

    4. Virginia

92. The first intercollegiate football game was played in New Brunswick; Rutgers College played Princeton. Rutgers won, in what year?

1. 1869	3. 1888
2. 1875	4. 1901

93. What is the state bug of New Jersey?

1. Wasps	3. Ants
2. Spider	4. Honeybee

94. The goldenrod was declared the state flower of Nebraska on April 4 of what year?

1. 1855
2. 1865
3. 1885
4. 1895

95. Nebraska is the only state in the union with a unicameral (one house) legislature. What does unicameral mean?

1. One House
2. Majority
3. Senate
4. House of representative

96. Marlon Brando's mother gave Henry Fonda acting lessons at what famous theater?

1. Ole Opry
2. Omaha community playhouse
3. Majestic Theater
4. Oriental Theater

DID YOU KNOW: The state of Texas was an independent nation from 1836 to 1845

97. The Confederate flag was designed and first flown in Alabama in what year?
1. 1852
2. 1868
3. 1861
4. 1888

98. In which of these was a skeleton of a prehistoric man was found?
1. Colossal Cave
2. Russell Cave
3. Boyden Cave
4. Spring Cave

99. Which of these governors served four terms in office?
1. Nelson Rockefeller
2. Cecil Andrus
3. George Wallace
4. James Rhodes

100. Huntsville, Alabama is known as the <u>xxxxx</u> capital of the world?
1. Pecan
2. Tree
3. Fish
4. Rocket

DID YOU KNOW: In 1882 the first hydroelectric plant in the United States was built at Fox River, Wisconsin

5 HARD

101. What is a jicama?
  1. Cuban Tahd
  2. Mexican Yam
  3. Brazilian Ginger
  4. Jamaican Potato

102. Who wrote the American literary classic The Scarlet Letter?
  1. F. Scott Fitzgerald
  2. Edgar Allen Poe
  3. Stephen King
  4. Nathaniel Hawthorne

103. In what year did Alaska officially became the property of the United States?
  1. 1889
  2. 1867
  3. 1901
  4. 1926

104. How much did money did United States Secretary of State, William H. Seward offer Russia for Alaska, which comes out to .02 cents per acre?
  1. 7.2M
  2. 2.6M
  3. 3.9M
  4. 8.4M

DID YOU KNOW: The state of Virginia was named for England's "Virgin Queen," Elizabeth I

105. The State motto of Alaska is?
1. North to Russia
2. Home of the bears
3. North to the future
4. Success is born here

106. Google's new KitKat operating system is designed for which kind of smartphones?
1. Android
2. Iphone
3. Windows
4. Blackberry

107. Hatch, New Mexico is known as the "xxx capital of the world?"

1. Enchilada	3. Burrito
2. Green Chile	4. Taco

108. In what year was the National Fire Safety symbol Smokey the Bear was found trapped in a tree when his home in Lincoln National Forest was destroyed by fire?
1. 1948
2. 1982
3. 1950
4. 1963

DID YOU KNOW: Polo was played for the first time in the United States in 1876.

109. Who was actor Clark Gable married to at the time of his death?

1. Carole Lombard
2. Kay Williams
3. Sylvia Ashley
4. Josephene Dillon

110. Actress-singer Polly Bergen, from Knoxville, is the first woman to serve on the Board of Directors of what major Company?

1. Palmolive Corp
2. Hoover Vacuum
3. Singer Sewing Machine
4. Ford Motor Company

111. Who was the only person in American history to be both an Admiral in the Navy and a General in the Army?

1. Chester Nimitz
2. Samuel Powhatan Carter
3. George S. Patton
4. Dwight D. Eisenhower

112. Who was the first woman United States Senator?

1. Hattie Caraway
2. Claire McCaskill
3. Elizabeth Dole
4. Patty Murray

DID YOU KNOW: The Redwood Library and Athenaeum in Newport , Rhode Island is the United States' oldest library building

113. The largest earthquake in American history, the New Madrid Earthquake occurred in the winter of 1811-12 in what state?

    1. New Mexico

    2. California

    3. Louisiana

    4. Tennessee

114. What building houses The National Civil Rights Museum in Memphis? Where incidentally Dr. Martin Luther King, Jr. was slain in 1968. The museum preserves and tells the history of the American Civil Rights Movement.

    1. Museum of nation history

    2. Lorraine Motel

    3. FBI Building

    4. Standard Oil Building

115. Which was the first state to give women the right to vote?

    1. Wyoming

    2. New York

    3. California

    4. Illinois

116. Which park is the first official national Park in the USA?

    1. Yosemite

    2. Hot Springs

    3. Yellowstone

    4. Shenandoah

DID YOU KNOW: The state of Virginia has had 3 capital cities: Jamestown, Williamsburg, and

Richmond.

117. What is the name of the largest coal mine in the United States?
    1. Black Thunder
    2. Black Gold
    3. Coal Creek
    4. Falkirk

118. The JCPenny department stores was originally started in what location?
Santa Ana, California
Kemmerer, Wyoming
Milwaukee, Wisconsin
Columbus, Ohio

119. Which State is nicknamed "the badger state?"
    1. Virginia
    2. Wisconsin
    3. North Dakota
    4. Iowa

120. The original Barbie is from Willows, Wisconsin. What is Barbie's full name?
    1. Barbie Hattie McCoy
    2. Barbie Gertrude Smith
    3. Barbie Esnah Braun
    4. Barbie Millicent Roberts

121. In what year was the first Ringling Brothers Circus staged in Baraboo, Wisconsin?

1. 1876   3. 1905
2. 1899   4. 1884

122. Where is home of Harley Davidson Motorcycles?

1. Chicago, Illinois
2. Indianapolis, Indiana
3. St. Paul, Minnesota
4. Milwaukee, Wisconsin

123. In the United States, where is the Hamburger hall of fame located?

1. Oakbrook, Illinois
2. Albany, New York
3. Boston, Massachusetts
4. Seymour, Wisconsin

124. Green Bay, Wisconsin has what notorious world's title?

1. Toliet Paper Capital
2. Football Capital
3. Skiing Capital
4. Cheese Capital

125. Located on the Back Fork of the Elk River in Webster Springs. West Virginia, is a world's largest tree, what type is it?

1. Sycamore   3. Pine
2. Redwood   4. Spruce

DID YOU KNOW: Captain John Smith named New Hampshire after the town of Hampshire, England

6 SPICY HOT

126. Which is the only state in the Union to have acquired its sovereignty by proclamation of the President of the United States?

    1. Alaska

    2. West Virginia

    3. Guam

    4. Hawaii

127. Which of these was not born in West Virginia?

    1. Shirley Temple

    2. Don Knotts

    3. Mary Lou Retton

    4. Chuck Yeager

128. In what year was the original Grimes Golden Apple Tree was discovered near Wellsburg?

    1. 1872

    2. 1775

    3. 1888

    4. 1828

129. What is the name given to the largest and oldest white oak tree in the United States that on September 10, 1938, was declared dead and felled with a ceremony?

    1. Mighty Oak

    2. Bunyon Oak

    3. Great Oak

    4. Mingo Oak

130. In what year was the first brick street in the world laid in Charleston, West Virginia, on Summers Street, between Kanawha and Virginia Streets?

1. 1825
2. 1836
3. 1870
4. 1896

131. Not including the union territories, how many states does India have?

1. 7
2. 28
3. 12
4. 13

132. In 1814 the French was defeated by allies (Britain, Austria, Russia, Prussia, Sweden, and Portugal) in War of Liberation. Where was Napoleon exiled?

1. Corsica
2. Elba
3. The isle of wright
4. Malta

133. In what year was slavery abolished in the British Empire?

1. 1865
2. 1735
3. 1788
4. 1833

DID YOU KNOW: Benjamin Franklin founded the Philadelphia Zoo, the first public zoo in the United States

134. In 1008 Murasaki Shikibu finishes a novel titled?
    1. The Tale of Genji
    2. The seven samurai
    3. The other woman
    4. Heavens gate

135. According to Shakespeare play MACBETH; in the year 1040, Macbeth murders which king?
    1. Louis VII
    2. Duncan
    3. Richard
    4. Eric

136. During the years 1150-1167, what famous international university was founded?
    1. London
    2. Berlin
    3. Chicago
    4. Oxford

137. In what century was the Mona Lisa thought to have been painted?

    1. Twentieth
    2. Nineteen
    3. Seventeen
    4. Sixteen

DID YOU KNOW: The city of Santa Fe, New Mexico is the highest capital city in the United States at 7,000 feet above sea level.

138. How many holes are there on a standard Chinese checkers board?

    1. 103   3. 156

    2. 75   4. 121

139. Which state produces more apples than any other state in the United States of America?

    1. Michigan

    2. Washington

    3. New York

    4. Virginia

140. In the USA ,in what year was the first revolving restaurant built?

    1. 1961

    2. 1965

    3. 1968

    4. 1970

141. Which is the only state to be named after a United States president.

    1. Virginia

    2. Washington

    3. Tennessee

    4. Alabama

142. What is the capital city of the state of Washington?

    1. Seattle

    2. Spokane

    3. Olympia

    4. Redmond

DID YOU KNOW: Passaic river in New Jersey was the site to the first submarine ride by inventor John P. Holland.

143. The oldest operating gas station in the United States is located in?
  1. Lincoln, Nebraska
  2. Springfield, Virginia
  3. Boston, Massachusetts
  4. Zillah, Washington

144. Starbucks, the biggest coffee chain in the world was founded in?
  1. New York, New York
  2. Seattle, Washington
  3. Chicago, Illinois
  4. Milwaukee, Wisconsin

145. Washington became the 42nd state in the United States on November 11 of what year?
  1. 1849
  2. 1899
  3. 1889
  4. 1866

146. Which of these innovative Internet companies, was not founded in Washington State?
  1. Amazon.com
  2. Google
  3. Classmates.com
  4. Whitepages.com

DID YOU KNOW: State of Washington Residents are called "Washingtonians" (emphasis on the third syllable, pronounced as tone).

147. Which of these states does NOT levy personal income tax
1. Illinois
3. Nevada
2. Florida
4. Alaska

148. United Airlines was originally owned by what company?
1. American
2. Airbus
3. Boeing
4. McDonnel Douglas

149. Popular games Pictionary, Pickle-ball, and Cranium were all invented in which State?
1. Kansas
2. Washington
3. New York
4. Alaska

150. Microsoft Corporation is located in Redmond. Where does Bill Gates Live?
1. Spookane
2. Seattle
3. Medina
4. Olympia

DID YOU KNOW: The state of arkansas official state beverage is milk. It was designated in 1985.

Book of Grand Trivia

7 FEEL THE BURN

151. The Hollywood Walk of Fame is located on the intersection of Hollywood Blvd and which other street?
1. Oak
2. Vine
3. Mape
4. Cedar

152. Which state are Krispy Kreme doughnuts originally from?

1. New York
2. North Carolina
3. New Jersey
4. Florida

153. Arizona leads the United States in the production of what metal?
1. Iron
2. Aluminum
3. Copper
4. Tin

154. The battleship USS Arizona was named in honor of the state. It was commissioned in 1913 and launched in?
1. 1913
2. 1914
3. 1915
4. 1917

DID YOU KNOW: The sum of the digits of any number which is a multiple of 9 is always 9 , eg 27,45,54..etc..

155. The original London Bridge was shipped stone-by-stone and reconstructed in what USA city?

    1. Lake Havasu City

    2. Brooklyn City

    3. Virginia City

    4. Fargo

156. In 1939 architect Frank Lloyd Wright's studio, Taliesin West, was built near what major City?

    1. Chicago, Illinois

    2. Phoenix, Arizona

    3. Detroit, Michigan

    4. San Francisco, California

157. The Hopis Indians founded the oldest Indian settlement in the United States named?

    1. Navajo

    2. Cherokee

    3. Oraibi

    4. Kree

158. Where is the world's largest solar telescope located at in the city of Sells?

    1. Herrett Observatory

    2. Kitts Peak national Observatory

    3. Gen D. Riley Observatory

    4. Dark Sky Observatory

DID YOU KNOW: In 2014, the city of Atlanta was paralysed by a mere 3 inches of snowfall

159. In what year did Arizona become the 48th State?
1. 1865
2. 1888
3. 1912
4. 1901

160. The term "Four Corners" is noted as a spot where?
1. A person can get the best Italian food
2. A person can see 4 stars aligned
3. An intersection consisting of the 4 tallest building in the world
4. A place where a person can stand in four states at the same time

161. What famous cemetery whose gravesites are those of Al Jolson, George Jessel, Eddie Canter, Jack Benny, and Percy Faith?

1. Oakwood   3. Graceland

2. Hillside   4. Woodlawn

162. San Bernardino County is the largest county in the country. Approx how many acres does it have?
1. 4 million
2. 2-million
3. 6 million
4. 3 million

DID YOU KNOW: The Ozark National Forest in Arkansas covers more than one million acres

163. In 1960 the first person to personally receive a star on the Walk of Fame in Hollywood was?

    1. Jack Benny
    2. Rock Hudson
    3. Joanne Woodward
    4. Natalie Wood

164. What is the name of the marble that gives the Colorado State Capitol its distinctive splendor. Cutting, polishing, and installing the marble in the Capitol took six years, from 1894 to 1900. All of that type marble in the world went into the Capitol. It cannot be replaced, at any price.

    1. Ashford Black Marble
    2. Beulah Red
    3. Rosa Aurora
    4. Red Verona

165. What is the name of the world's largest flat top mountain?

    1. Grand Mesa
    2. Tucucari Mountain
    3. Table Mountain
    4. Glass Mountain

166. Denver, lays claim to the invention of the cheeseburger. The trademark for the name Cheeseburger was awarded in 1935 to whom?

    1. Herr Burger
    2. Johannes Burger
    3. Louis Ballast
    4. Ronald McDonald

167. What is the longest continuous street in America?
  1. Irving Park Rd, Chicago, Illinois
  2. Colfax Avenue in Denver, Colorado
  3. Figueroa Street, Los Angeles California
  4. Mac Corkle Ave., Charleston WV.

168. What town and state has the title of the "Pinto Bean" capital of the world?
  1. Tucucarie, New Mexico
  2. Boca Raton, Florida
  3. Laredo, Texas
  4. Dove Creek, Colorado

169. John Henry "Doc" Holliday's brief and tumultuous existence led him to Glenwood Springs where he succumbed to tuberculosis and died at the Hotel Glenwood in what year?
  1. 1862
  2. 1868
  3. 1877
  4. 1887

170. In the United States, what is the only state that grows coffee commercially?
  1. Hawaii
  2. North Carolina
  3. Colorado
  4. New York

DID YOU KNOW: Thailand was established in the mid-14th century and known as Siam until 1939

171. What is the windiest city in the United States?
　　1. Chicago, Illinois
　　2. Dodge City, Kansas
　　3. New York, New York
　　4. St Paul, Minnesota

172. Who was the first black woman to win an Academy Award?
　　1. Dorothy Dandridge
　　2. Diahann Carroll
　　3. Ethel Waters
　　4. Hatie McDaniel

173. The American Institute of Baking is located in Manhattan, _?
　　1. New York
　　2. Illinois
　　3. Kansas
　　4. California

174. What magazine did DeWitt Wallace start while recovering from injuries after WWI?
　　1. Time
　　2. Readers Digest
　　3. Life
　　4. Mad

DID YOU KNOW:Brazil is the largest country in South America; sharing common boundaries with every South American country except Chile and Ecuador

175. What is the smallest state in size in the United States?
1. Maine
2. Connecticut
3. Rhode Island
4. Delaware

8 GETTING HARD

176. Rhode Island was home to the first National Lawn Tennis Championship in what year?
1. 1912
2. 1910
3. 1901
4. 1899

177. What name is given to a 11 ft tall, gold-covered, bronze statue placed atop the State House on December 18, 1899 in the state of Rhode Island?
1. Paul Bunyon
2. Pioneer Woman
3. Independent Man
4. Burning Man

178. What is the name of the oldest operating tavern in the United States?
1. Bell in Hand tavern
2. The White Horse tavern
3. Longfellow's wayside Inn
4. Tun Tavern

DID YOU KNOW: In the United States,Philadelphia is the site of the first presidential mansion

179. Rhode Island founder Roger Williams established the First Baptist Church in America?
1. Thomas Jefferson
2. Thomas Greene
3. Roger Williams
4. Padre Eusebio Kino

180. Built in 1763 ,what synagogue houses the oldest torah in North America?
1. Kahal Kadosh Beth Elohim
2. Kahal Kadosh beth Shalom
3. Touro
4. B'nai Israel Temple

181. What nationality was 19th century writer Sir Walter Scott?
1. Irish
2. Scottish
3. Dutch
4. English

182. Approximately how much does a liter of water weigh?
1. 700 Grams
2. 1 Pound
3. 1 Kilogram
4. 18 Ounces

DID YOU KNOW: The state of Georgia is the nations number one producer of the three Ps--peanuts, pecans, and peaches.

183. The world famous "Mardi Gras" is celebrated in what US city?

1. Los Angeles
3. New Orleans
2. New York
4. Chicago

184. Louisiana was named in honor of what famous person?

1. Robert Louis Stevenson
2. King Louis XIV
3. Saint Louis
4. Louis Jolliet

185. Louisiana is the only state in the union that does not have counties , what are they called?

1. Buroughs
2. Parrishes
3. Subdivisions
4. Loudivs

186. The Acadians were driven out of Canada in the 1700s because they wouldn't pledge allegiance to the King of England. What are their descendants called?

1. Cajuns
2. Romans
3. Steelers
4. Ottomans

187. The first American army to have African American officers was called?

1. Tuskegee Corps
2. 332nd fighter group
3. The Corps d'Afrique
4. African American Corps

188. What does the phrase "Cannes Brulee" means?

 1. Canned Food   3. Festival of Cannes

 2. Quick soup   4. Burnt Canes

189. In what year did the United States purchase 'the Louisiana territory' from France?

 1. 1799

 2. 1803

 3. 1844

 4. 1862

190. How much did United States pay France for "the Louisiana territory?"

 1. 7 Million

 2. 10 Million

 3. 15 Million

 4. 25 Million

191. How many states comprise "the Louisiana territory?"

 1. 1

 2. 5

 3. 8

 4. 13

192. Name only state in the United States whose name has one syllable?

 1. Utah

 2. Ohio

 3. Iowa

 4. Maine

DID YOU KNOW: In Idaho state law forbids a citizen to give another citizen a box of candy that weighs more than 50 pounds.

193. Which of these is Maine not the largest producer of?

1. Wheat
2. Lobster

3. Blueberries
4. Toothpicks

194. Harare is the capital of which country?

1. Tanzania
2. Zimbabwe
3. Zambia
4. Ghana

195. What is Rick's nightclub called in the movie Casablanca?

1. Copacabana
2. Rick's cafe American
3. Billy goat cafe
4. Me Casa su Casa

196. Which of these are not among the works of Henry Wadsworth Longfellow?

1. The courtship of miles Standish
2. Hiawatha
3. Great Expectations
4. Evangelene

197. Which state's blueberry crop is the largest in the nation?

1. Nebraska
2. Maine
3. Virginia
4. Kentucky

DID YOU KNOW: The first successful parachute jump to be made from a moving airplane was made by

Captain Berry in 1912

198. Which of these is the largest state in area
  1. Vermont   3. Maine
  2. Connecticut   4. Massachusetts

199. Montpelier, Vermont is the only state capital in the nation that does not have a _?
  1. JC Pennys
  2. Meadow Mart
  3. Subway
  4. McDonalds

200. Which state is the largest producer of maple syrup in the U.S.?
  1. Kentucky
  2. Vermont
  3. Indiana
  4. New Hampshire

DID YOU KNOW: Soda Springs ,Idaho boasts the largest man-made geyser in the world.

9 INSANE HARD

201. Who was the only US president to have a birthday on 4th July?
1. Calvin Coolidge
2. Abraham Lincoln
3. John Kennedy
4. George Washington

202. Of the thirteen original colonies, which colony was the first to declare its independence from Mother England -- a full six months before the Declaration of Independence was signed?
1. Delaware
2. Maryland
3. New Hampshire
4. New Jersey

203. New Hampshire adopted the first legal lottery in the twentieth century United States in what year?
1. 1956
2. 1975
3. 1979
4. 1963

DID YOU KNOW:The number 40 when written "forty" is the only number with letters in alphabetical order

204. Who invented the first alarm clock in 1787?
1. Thomas Edison
2. Levi Hutchins
3. Nikola Tesla
4. Benjamin Franklin

205. Who was the first sculptor to design an American coin?
1. Daniel Chester French
2. Augustus Saint-Gaudens
3. Man Ray
4. Alexander Calder

206. Who designed the four bas-reliefs in the Memorial Bell Tower at Cathedral of the Pines in Rindge?
1. Pablo Picasso
2. Jean Renoir
3. John Turner
4. Norman Rockwell

207. New Hampshire's state motto is "Live Free or Die". The motto comes from a statement written by which Revolutionary Major General?
1. Nathanael Greene
2. John Stark
3. Robert Howe
4. Henry Knox

DID YOU KNOW: In Pacific Grove, California, there

is a law on the books establishing a $500 fine for molesting butterflies

208. Who wrote the poem "Mary Had a Little Lamb" in 1830?

    1. Charles Dickens

    2. Henry Wadsworth Longfellow

    3. Sarah Josepha Hale

    4. Ralph Waldo Emerson

209. Approximately how many gallons of sap does it take to make approximately 1 gallon of maple syrup?

    1. 30

    2. 40

    3. 45

    4. 55

210. When was the first subway system built in the United States?

    1. 1920

    2. 1888

    3. 1901

    4. 1897

211. What is the original name for the game we now call "volleyball?"

    1. Cricket   3. Senet

    2. Mintonette   4. Vollenette

212. Who is the inventor of the first liquid fueled rocket?

    1. Albert Einstein

    2. Nikola Tesla

3. Robert Goddard

4. George Edward Alcorn

213. The birth control pill was invented at which of these schools?

1. University of Illinois

2. Yale

3. Michigan State

4. Clark University

214. What was the first college established in North America?

1. Yale

2. Harvard

3. University of Chicago

4. Michigan Institute if Technology

215. Presidents John Adams and John Quincy Adams are buried in the crypt at what church?

1. United First Parish Church

2. St Stephens Church

3. Hall of American Saints

4. Our lady of Missions

216. What is an adult male polar bear known as?

1. Buck

2. Boar

3. King

4. Sow

DID YOU KNOW: The town of Milton, Delaware was named after the English poet John Milton in 1807

217. MLB baseballs are made in Costa Rica and pro basketballs are made in China. Where in the world are NFL footballs made?
1. China
2. India
3. United States
4. Argentina

218. The Boston Tea Party reenactment takes place in Boston Harbor every?
1. November12th
2. December 16th
3. November 22nd
4. December 12th

219. Charles Goodyear in Woburn first vulcanized rubber in?
1. 1901
2. 1882
3. 1910
4. 1839

220. Who invented the first sewing machine in 1845?
1. Josef Madersperger
2. Elias Howe
3. Walter Hunt
4. Isaac Singer

DID YOU KNOW: Babe Ruth hit his first home run in Fayetteville,North Carolina on March 7, 1914.

221. The first Thanksgiving Day in the United Sates was celebrated in Plymouth in?

    1. 1611   3. 1621

    2. 1635   4. 1701

222. What is the name of the world's first nuclear powered submarine?

    1. USS HARTFORD

    2. USS NAUTILUS

    3. USS TOLEDO

    4. USS VIRGINIA

223. The first telephone book ever issued had how many names?

    1. 50

    2. 100

    3. 150

    4. 300

224. The New Haven District Telephone Company published the first telephone book in what year?

    1. 1899

    2. 1902

    3. 1878

    4. 1870

225. In Hartford, Connecticut, you may not, under any circumstances, __.

1. Walk the street with more than 2 dogs
2. Eat Ice Cream on a Monday
3. Hula hoop on a public road
4. Cross the street walking on your hands

10 INSANITY

226. Which wrestling association is headquartered in Stamford, Connecticut?
    1. NWA   3. AWA
    2. WWF   4. CWA

227. Who is the author of the first dictionary published in 1807?
    1. Noah Webster
    2. Ladislav Zgusta
    3. Henry George Liddell
    4. Robert Scott

228. Who is known to have made the first friction matches in Beacon Falls in 1834?
    1. John Walker
    2. Robert Boyle
    3. Joshua Pusey
    4. Thomas Sanford

229. Which is the only state without any National Park System units such as national parks, historic sites, memorials and battlefields?
    1. Maine
    2. South Dakota
    3. Delaware

4. Georgia

DID YOU KNOW: The Methodist Church of America was formally organized in 1784

230. Who invented the automatic flour-milling machinery that revolutionized the industry?
1. Oliver Evans
2. Richard Ferrel
3. General Mills
4. C.H. Guenther

231. Who invented Coca-Cola?
1. Caleb Bradham
2. Dr John Pemberton
3. Charles Aderton
4. Barney Hartman

232. In what year was "Coca-Cola " invented?
1. 1868
2. 1876
3. 1886
4. 1896

233. What is the official state flower for the state of Georgia?
1. Peach Blossom
2. Apple Blossom
3. Scarlet Carnation
4. Cherokee Rose

234. The figures of Stonewall Jackson, Jefferson Davis, and Robert E. Lee make up the world's largest sculpture. It is located on the face of?

1. Rock Mountain
2. Stone Mountain
3. Mount Jefferson
4. Tower Mountain

235. What did the Packard Motor Car Company in Detroit manufacture in 1939?

1. First air conditioned car
2. First car with power brakes
3. First car with a radio
4. First car reclining seats

236. The state of Michigan is the only place in the world with?

1. A two headed dog
2. Flying automobile
3. A floating post office
4. Upside down house

237. What is the name given to the largest crucifix in the world?

1. Lords sign
2. Remember me
3. Arisen
4. Cross in the woods

238. What flavor liqueur is Cointreau?

1. Orange
2. Peach
3. Mint
4. Strawberry

DID YOU KNOW: Key West, Florida has the highest average temperature in the United States

239. What is the name the first department store in the States?
1. Sears and Roebuck
2. LL Bean
3. Zions Co-operative Mercantile Institution
4. Goldblatts department stores

240. The Uinta mountain range is named after?
1. Wintu
2. Umatilla
3. Yakima
4. Ute

241. Utah was acquired by the United States in the treaty ending the Mexico War in what year?
1. 1862
2. 1855
3. 1848
4. 1866

242. Which state has the highest literacy rate in the nation?
1. Illinois
2. Utah
3. New York
4. Massachusetts

243. Texas is popularly known as?
1. The long horn state
2. The lone star state

3. The cowboy state

4. The oil state

DID YOU KNOW: The world's largest shrimp is on display at the Old Spanish Fort Museum in Pascagoula, Mississippi

244. The King Ranch in Texas is bigger than which of these states?

1. Massachusetts   3. Connecticut

2. Delaware   4. Rhode Island

245. What is the only state to enter the United States by treaty instead of territorial annexation?

1. Texas

2. Utah

3. New Mexico

4. Colorado

246. What is the name of the only natural lake in the state of Texas?

1. Lake Austin

2. Caddo Lake

3. Lake Houston

4. Lake Placid

247. What is the capital of Texas?

1. Austin

2. Dallas

3. Houston

4. San Antonio

248. What is the world's largest inland port?

1. Memphis

2. St Louis

3. Laredo
4. Pittsburgh

DID YOU KNOW: The International Checkers Hall of Fame is in Petal, Mississippi

249. Where do you find the world's largest helium well?
1. Salt lake City, Utah
2. Sidney, Australia
3. Montreal, Canada
4. Amarillo, Texas

250. What is the state dance of South Carolina called?
1. Square dance
2. Shag
3. Irish Dance
4. Hokey Pokey

DID YOU KNOW: Pine Sol was invented in 1929 by Harry A. Cole, Sr

11 ULTIMATE

251. Who was the Sculptor who began drilling into the 6,200-foot Mount Rushmore in 1927?
1. Charles Despiau
2. Jacob Epstein
3. Gutzon Borglum
4. Ernest Gillick

252. Which U.S. President purchased the Louisiana Territory from France, a real-estate deal that at the time doubled the size of the United States?
1. John Adams
2. James Monroe
3. Thomas Jefferson
4. John Quincy Adams

253. Wind Cave in South Dakota, contains the world's largest display of a rare formation called?
1. Boxwork
2. Flowstone

3. Shelfstone

4. Stalactite

DID YOU KNOW: Ermal Fraze invented the pop-top can

254. What is the name of the most endangered land mammal in North America?
1. Gray Wolf
2. Black-Footed ferret
3. Narwhal
4. Beavers

255. Where do you find the home of the world's only Corn Palace?
1. Murdo, South Dakota
2. Minot, North Dakota
3. Mitchell, South Dakota
4. McPherson, Kansas

256. The largest underground gold mine is called?
1. LaRonde Mine
2. Conco Mine
3. Wildman Mines
4. Homestake Mines

257. Which is the most decorated battleship during World War II?
1. USS Iowa
2. USS South Dakota
3. USS Arizona

4. USS Washington

258. Newton Hills State Park, south of Canton, South Dakota is part of a geological feature called the Coteau des Prairie. What created this?
    1. Erosion   3. Glaciers
    2. Waterways   4. Earthquake

259. In what year did North Dakota pass a bill in 1987 making English the official state language?
    1. 1987
    2. 1972
    3. 1965
    4. 1951

260. Dakota is a Sioux word meaning?
    1. Buffalo
    2. Water
    3. Friends
    4. Food

261. How long did Queen Victoria's reign?
    1. 64
    2. 54
    3. 50
    4. 42

262. In 1903 the Wright Brothers made the first successful powered flight by man at what location near Kitty Hawk?
    1. Eagle Point
    2. Devils Mound
    3. Kill Devil Hill

4. Old man bluff

DID YOU KNOW: W.F. Semple patented chewing gum in 1869.

263. Transylvania County is home to the highest waterfall in the eastern United States. What is the name of the waterfall?
1. Hatteras Falls
2. Sinister Falls
3. Colonial Falls
4. Whitewater Falls

264. North Carolina is the largest producer of what crop in the nation?
1. Blueberries
2. Sweet Potatoes
3. Corn
4. Soy Bean

265. The first English colony in America was located on Roanoke Island. Walter Raleigh founded it. The colony mysteriously vanished with no trace except for the a word scrawled on a nearby tree. What is that word?
1. Devilish
2. Arkadian
3. Croatoan
4. Wendigoe

266. What is the name of the slot machine invented by Charles Fey in 1899?
1. Liberty Bell
2. Sizzling Sevens
3. Lady Luck
4. Riverboat Queen

DID YOU KNOW: Cleveland, Ohio is home to the Rock and Roll Hall of Fame.

267. What is the name of Bugsy Siegel Las Vegas Casino?
1. The Pelican
2. The Flamingo
3. The Mirage
4. The Palace

268. How old was Bertha, a performing elephant at John Ascuaga's casino, when she died?
1. 26
2. 48
3. 52
4. 36

269. In Death Valley, what animal can live its entire life without drinking a drop of liquid?
1. Kangaroo Rat
2. Grey Goose
3. Black Rattle Snake
4. Desert Cat

270. St. Augustine Church in Nevada, requires the establishment's bells in the tower to be rung by pulling a rope located in?
1. The Lobby

2. The Pulpit
3. The Men's Restroom
4. The Kitchen

DID YOU KNOW: Long jumper DeHart Hubbard was the first African American to earn an Olympic Gold Medal during the 1924 Olympics games held in Paris. He set the record for long jumping then

271. Nevada takes its name from a Spanish word meaning?
    1. Desert Storm   3. Hurricane
    2. Snow Clad   4. Flood Waters

272. In the United States, which state has more mountain ranges than any other state?
    1. Pennsylvania
    2. Virginia
    3. West Virginia
    4. Nevada

273. At Lake Tahoe's Crystal Bay. It is possible to stand in both Nevada and California inside Cal-Neva's building. Which celebrity owned this unique building?
    1. Billy Crystal
    2. Frank Sinatra
    3. Howard Hughes
    4. Bugsy Siegel

274. Who was the first to say 'Holy Cow' during a baseball broadcast?
    1. Halsey Hal

2. Harry Caray
3. Vin Scully
4. Ernie Harwell

DID YOU KNOW: There is a house in Rockport, Massachusetts built entirely of newspaper

275. Which is the only facility in the country to host a Super Bowl, a World Series and a NCAA Final Four Basketball Championship?
1. Rosemont Horizon
2. Louisiana Superdome
3. Metrodome
4. Edward Jones Dome

DID YOU KNOW: Minneapolis ,Minnesota has more golfers per capita than any other city in the country

12 THE LAST 25

276. The nation's first Better Business Bureau was founded in Minneapolis in?

    1. 1926   3.1911

    2. 1929   4. 1912

277. The first open heart surgery and the first bone marrow transplant in the United States were done at the?

    1. University of Chicago

    2. University of Minnesota

    3. Michigan Institute of Technology

    4. Harvard

278. The first Automatic Pop-up toaster was marketed in June 1926 by McGraw Electric Co. in Minneapolis under the name Toastmaster. What was the retail price?

    1. $5.98

    2. $9.98

3. $13.50

4. $21.50

279. Candy maker Frank C. Mars of Minnesota introduced the Milky Way candy bar in what year?

1. 1930

2. 1923

3. 1937

4. 1918

DID YOU KNOW: The birth control pill was invented at Clark University in Worcester, Massachusetts

280. In 1898, the Kensington Rune stone was found on the farm of Olaf Ohman, near Alexandria, Minnesota. What story does The Kensington Rune stone carvings allegedly tell?

1. Space Aliens Landing

2. The journey of a band of Vikings

3. Battle between Cowboys and Indians

4. An angel visiting a child

281. There are only two states in the United States without self serve gas stations. New Jersey is one, what's the other?

1. Maryland

2. Kansas

3. Oregon

4. Wyoming

282. What is the deepest lake in the United States and is formed in the remains of an ancient volcano?

1. Chelan Lake

2. Lake Tahoe

3. Lake Superior

4. Crater Lake

283. Which of these United States Presidents was not born in Ohio?

    1. Rutherford B. Hayes

    2. John Quincy

    3. Warren G. Harding

    4. William McKinley

DID YOU KNOW: The first Intercollegiate Basketball game in the US was played on February 9,1895.

284. Which state in United States has the fewest counties?

    1. Maine

    2. Oregon

    3. Delaware

    4. New Hampshire

285. Sam Walton started the Wal Mart stores in

    1. Bentonville   3. Newport

    2. Kingfisher   4. Little Rock

286. Where was the first McDonald's originally opened in?

    1. San Bernardino, California

    2. Des Plaines, Illinois

    3. Oak Brook, Illinois

    4. Los Angeles, California

287. The University of Chicago was first opened in?

    1. 1856

    2. 1866

3. 1882

4. 1892

288. The most powerful earthquake to strike the United States, centered in New Madrid, Missouri. Occurred in?

1. 1852

2. 1811

3. 1924

4. 1888

DID YOU KNOW: Jack McCall was tried, convicted and hanged in 1877 for the shooting of Wild Bill Hickok

289. What is the only North American gem to be included in the Crown Jewels of England?

1. Yogo Sapphire

2. Carolina Emerald

3. Green Diamond

4. Hawaiian Black Pearl

290. Pinocchio is Italian for?

1. Pine Tart

2. Pasta sauce

3. Pine Head

4. Pine Tree

291.HIPPOPOTOMONSTROSESQUIP-PEDALIOPHOBIA is?

1. The fear of Heights

2. The fear of Long Words

3. The fear of Short Words

4. The fear of Long-distances

292. Which of the following words is a palindrome?

1. fearsome
2. shortest
3. racecar
4. airplane

293. Who developed the first flush toilet in 1884?
    1. Thomas Crapper
    2. Ian Flushing
    3. William Pooper
    4. George B. Wipes

DID YOU KNOW: The first American chess tournament was held in New York in 1843.

294. During his lifetime, how many paintings did Vincent Van Gogh sell?
    1. One
    2. Five
    3. Ten
    4. Sixteen

294. There were about 300 bones in your body when you were born, but by the time you reach adulthood, how many do you have?
    1. 288   3. 245
    2. 268   4. 206

295. What is the only substance on earth that is lighter as a solid than a liquid?
    1. Hydrogen
    2. Water
    3. Iron
    4. Crude Oil

296. What is the actual shape of a raindrop?

1. Tear shaped
2. Round
3. Oval
4. no shape

297. Name of the only person to be struck by lightning seven times and survive them?

1. Ante Djindjic
2. Sophie Frost
3. Alice Svensson
4. Roy Sullivan

298. One inch of rain is equivalent to how many inches of snow?

1. 3
2. 5
3. 8
4. 10

299. In what year did Congress declare Thanksgiving a legal holiday?

1. 1926
2. 1941
3. 1950
4. 1966

300. Which of these songs was not originally written as a Christmas song?

1. Deck the Halls
2. Christmas Tree
3. 12 days of Christmas

4.   Jingle Bells

DID YOU KNOW: Joseph C. Gayetty invented toilet paper in 1857

THE ANSWERS

1. #32. #3   3. #3   4. #2

5. #36. #1   7. #1   8. #1-six

9. #310. #3   11. #2   12. #2

13. #4   14. #3   15. #1   16. #3

17. #1   18. #1   19. #1   20. #2   21. #2

22. #1   23. #2   24. #2   25. #1   26. #4

27. #2   28. #3   29. #2   30. #3   31. #3

32. #4   33. #1   34. #2   35. #3   36. #4

37. #2   38. #3   39. #1   40. #2   41.#3

42.#3   43. #3   44. #2   45. #2   46. #3

47. #3   48.#2   49. #2   50. #1   51. #2

52. #1   53.#1   54. #3   55. #2   56. #1

57. #3   58.# 4   59.#3   60.#4   61.#1

62.# 3   63.#3   64. #1   65.#3

66.#2   67.#4   68.#3   69.#4

70.#2   71.#4   72.#2   73.#1

74.#4   75.#3   76.#3   77.#4

78.#2   79.#2   80.#2   81.#1

81a.#3   82.#4   83.#2   84.#4

85.#1   86.#3   87.#3   88.#1

89.#3   90.#2   91.#3   92.#1

93.#4   94.#4   95.#1   96.#2

97.#3   98.#2   99.#3   100.#4

101.#2   102.#4   103.#2   104.#1   105.#3

106.#1   107.#2   108.#3   109.#2   110.#3

111.#2   112.#1   113.#4   114.#2   115.#1

116.#3   117.#1   118.#2   119.#2   120.#4

121.#4   122.#3   123.#3   124.#1   125.#1

126.#2   127.#1   128.#2   129.#4   130.#3

131.#2	132.#2	133.#4	134.#1	135.#2
136.#4	137.#4	138.#4	139.#2	140.#1
141.#2	142.#3	143.#4	144.#2	145.#3
146.#2	147.#1	148.#3	149.#2	150.#3
151.#2	152.#2	153.#3	154.#3	155.#1
156.#2	157.#3	158.#2	159.#3	160.#4
161.#2	162.#4	163.#3	164.#2	165.#1
166.#3	167.#2	168.#4	169.#4	170.#1
171.#2	172.#4	173.#3	174.#2	175.#3
176.#4	177.#3	178.#2	179.#3	180.#3
181.#2	182.#3	183.#3	184.#2	185.#2
186.#1	187.#3	188.#4	189.#2	190.#3

191.#4   192.#4   193.#1   194.#2   195.#2

196.#3   197.#2   198.#3   199.#4   200.#2

201.#1   202.#3   203.#4   204.#2   205.#2

206.#4   207.#2   208.#3   209.#2   210.#4

211.#2   212.#3   213.#4   214.#2   215.#1

216.#2   217.#3   218.#2   219.#4   220.#2

221.#3   222.#2   223.#1   224.#3   225.#4

226.#2   227.#1   228.#4   229.#3   230.#1

231.#2   232.#3   233.#4   234.#2   235.#1

236.#3   237.#4   238.#1   239.#3   240.#4

241.#3   242.#2   243.#2   244.#4   245.#1

246.#2   247.#1   248.#3   249.#4   250.#2

251.#3 252.#3 253.#1 254.#2 255.#3

256.#4 257.#2 258.#3 259.#1 260.#3

261.#1 262.#3 263.#4 264.#2 265.#3

266.#1 267.#2 268.#2 269.#1 270.#4

271.#2 272.#3 273.#2 274.#1 275.#3

276.#4 277.#2 278.#3 279.#2

280.#2 281.#3 282.#4 283.#2 284.#3

285.#1 286.#2 287.#4 288.#2 289.#1

290.#3 291.#2 292.#3 293.#1

294.#1 295.#2 296.#2 297.#4 298.#3

299.#2 300.#4

Peter Joseph